THIS I BELIEVE (THE CREED) 5
HEAVEN AND EARTH 17
BROKEN VESSELS (AMAZING GRACE) 27
NO OTHER NAME 38
DEPTHS 51
CALVARY 62
THANK YOU JESUS 71
ALL THINGS NEW 82
MY STORY 93
OUR FATHER 105
MOUNTAIN 116

WE ARE A CHURCH COMMITTED TO INSPIRING AND EMPOWERING THE AUTHENTIC WORSHIP OF JESUS AND RESOURCING THE BODY OF CHRIST.

There are numerous resources we as Hillsong make available including inspiring teaching and books by Brian & Bobbie Houston, curriculum content that can impact your children's, outreach and discipleship ministries, and of course music.
For more information visit hillsongmusic.com

WE ARE A CHURCH THAT BELIEVES IN CHAMPIONING THE CAUSE OF THE LOCAL CHURCH.

Hillsong Conference is about you, your church and seeing God's Kingdom advance across the earth. This is your chance to lean in, receive and take home practical teachings you can outwork in your own church home, family and community. It's about being refreshed and inspired and finding great strength and unity amongst the diversity of the local church worldwide. For more information visit hillsongconference.com

WE ARE A CHURCH THAT BELIEVES IN PLACING VALUE UPON WOMANHOOD.

Colour Conference... At the very core is a strong humanitarian message. Our passion and labour is to place value upon womanhood, so that we in turn can arise from a place of strength and cohesion and place value upon fellow humanity. For more information visit colourconference.com

WE ARE A CHURCH THAT BELIEVES IN REACHING AND INFLUENCING THE WORLD WITH THE MESSAGE OF JESUS CHRIST.

Hillsong Television with Brian Houston is a half-hour Christian television program that features his teaching from Hillsong Church services. Pastor Brian's messages are empowering, passionate and practical for everyday life. His teaching will inspire you with the hope, joy, meaning and purpose that can be found in a personal and loving God. For more information visit hillsongtv.com

WE ARE A CHURCH THAT BELIEVES IN PARTNERSHIP AND UNITY AS WE ADVANCE HIS KINGDOM ON EARTH.

The Hillsong Leadership Network is all about connecting, equipping and serving leaders, and exists to champion the cause of local churches everywhere. Our heart is that by coming alongside leaders, churches and ministries of varying denominations and styles, we are able to see more churches flourish and reach their God-given potential through this membership program. For more information visit hillsongnetwork.com

WE ARE A CHURCH THAT BELIEVES IN EQUIPPING PEOPLE WITH PRINCIPLES AND TOOLS TO LEAD AND IMPACT IN EVERY SPHERE OF LIFE.

To find further information about the Pastoral Leadership Streams (including Youth, Children, Event Management, or Social Justice Pathways), Creative Streams (including Worship Music, TV & Media, Dance, or Production) or a Degree Program offered on campus by Alphacrucis College visit hillsongcollege.com

WE ARE A CHURCH IN MANY LOCATIONS...

Sydney, Brisbane, Melbourne, London, Kiev, Cape Town, New York City, Los Angeles, Moscow, Stockholm, Paris, Konstanz, Düsseldorf, Copenhagen, Amsterdam, Barcelona
For service times and information visit hillsong.com

OUR PRAYER FOR YOU

Our prayer is that you would discover the author of love... the Lord Jesus Christ. His life and death represent the greatest gift of love the world will ever see... "This is real love - not that we loved God, but that he loved us and sent his Son as a sacrifice to take away our sins." 1 John 4:9-10 (NLT)... God paid the ultimate sacrifice sending His Son, Jesus Christ, who died on the cross in our place and rose again to prove His victory, restore our relationship with Him and empower us for life. It is through Jesus Christ that we can know and be reconciled with God... All we need to do is believe in Him and accept Jesus Christ as our Lord and Saviour. It is as simple as praying a prayer...asking Jesus to meet you right where you are... It is a brand new start of living in relationship with God... If you are not sure that you personally know the Lord Jesus, then can we encourage you to make this your prayer today...

Dear Lord Jesus, Thank you for dying on the cross for me. Thank you for your amazing love. I repent of my sins and thank you for your forgiveness. Please come into my life and give me a fresh start. I believe in you and accept you as my Lord and Saviour. I am now a Christian - a follower of Jesus Christ and you now live in me. Help me to live my life for you from this day forward. Amen.

If you have prayed this prayer today, we would love to hear from you! Please write to us at Hillsong Church, PO Box 1195, Castle Hill, NSW 1765, Australia or email us at prayer@hillsong.com

TERMS AND CONDITIONS

Thank you for purchasing sheet music from Hillsong Music. Your purchase grants you the right to make ONE copy of the sheet music for your personal purposes (performances, worship services, personal study, musical teaching, etc). However the following rights have NOT been granted to you:

1. Reproduce copies of the sheet music in whole or in part outside of the rights granted to you above.
2. To translate, enhance, modify, alter or adapt the sheet music or any part of it for any purpose.
3. Cause or permit any third party to translate, enhance, modify, alter or adapt the sheet music or any part of it for any purpose.
4. Sub-licence, lease, lend, sell, rent, distribute or grant others any rights, or provide copies of the sheet music to others. Reproductions of the sheet music can be made for the purpose of church worship only with an existing Music Reproduction Licence from CCLI. For further information contact CCLI at http://www.ccli.com

For further information about copyright or other use of this music, please contact Hillsong Music Publishing at publishing@hillsong.com

TRANSCRIBED & ENGRAVED BY JARED HASCHEK

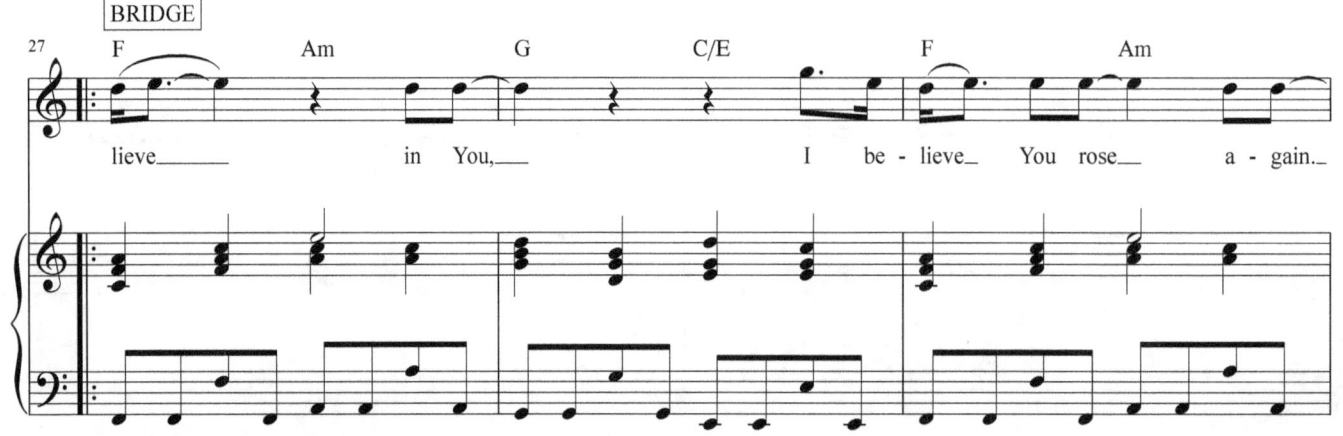

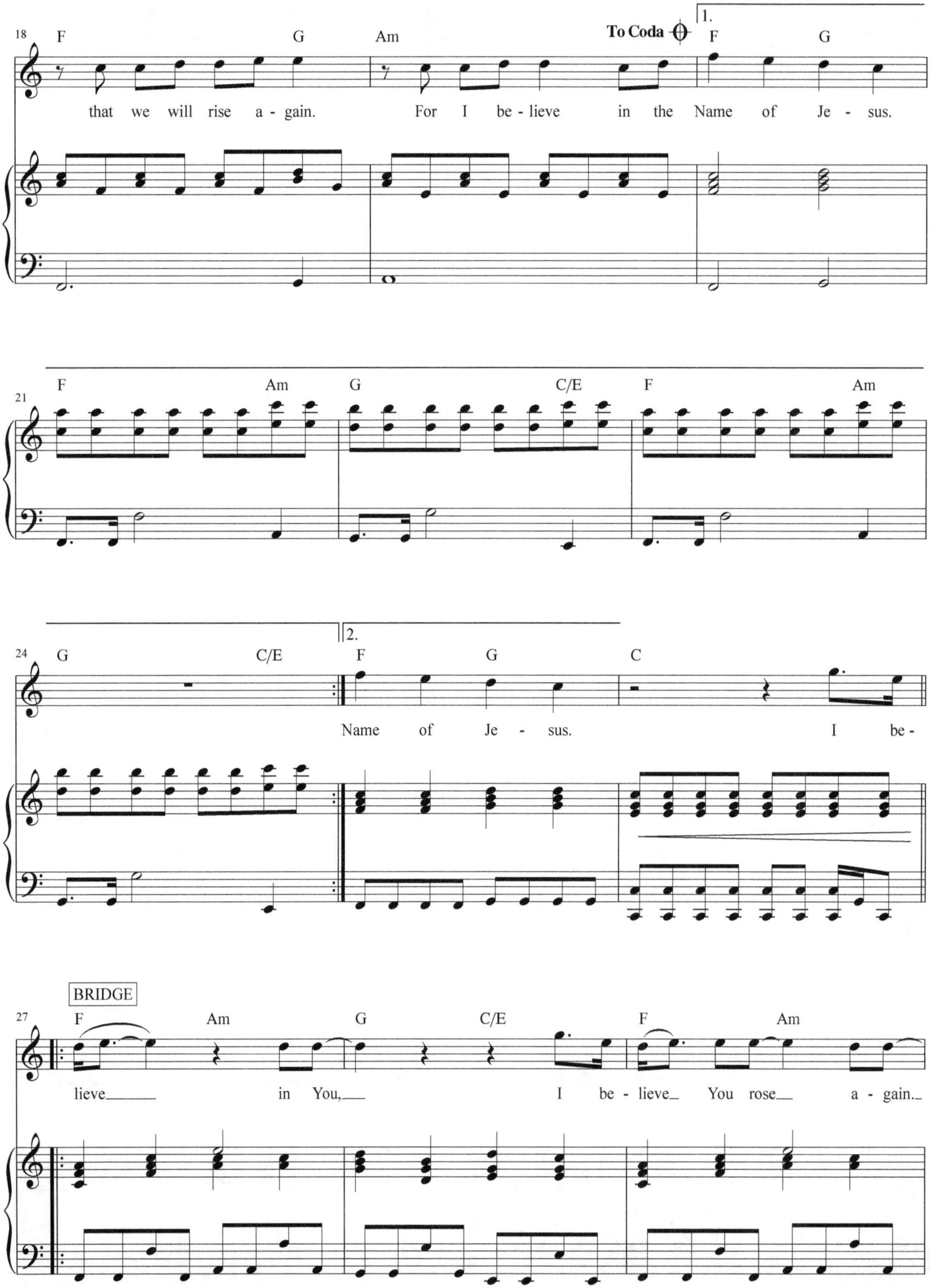
18
F G Am
To Coda
1.
F G
that we will rise a - gain. For I be - lieve in the Name of Je - sus.
21
F Am G C/E F Am
24
G C/E
2.
F G C
Name of Je - sus. I be -
BRIDGE
27
F Am G C/E F Am
lieve in You, I be - lieve You rose a - gain.

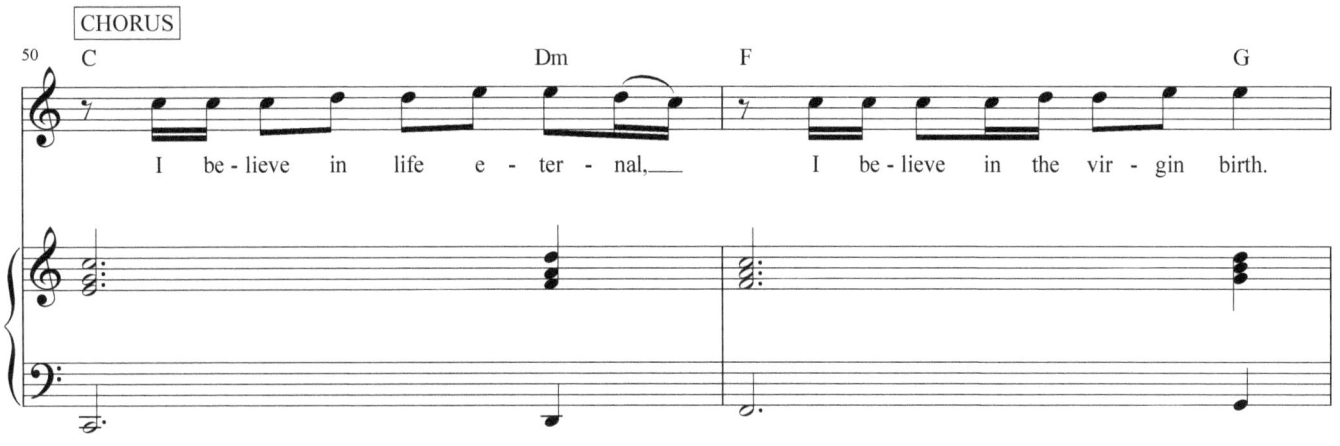
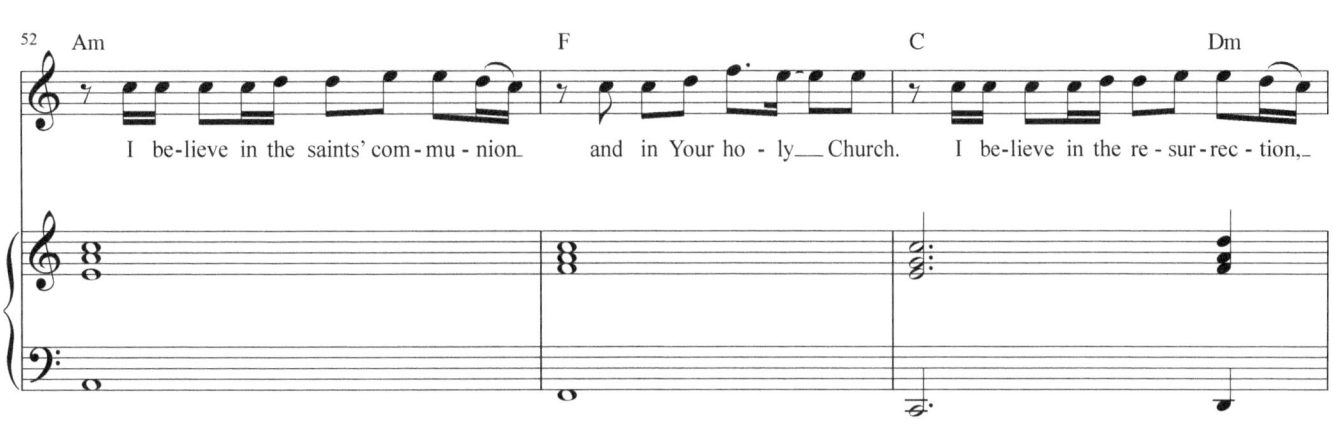
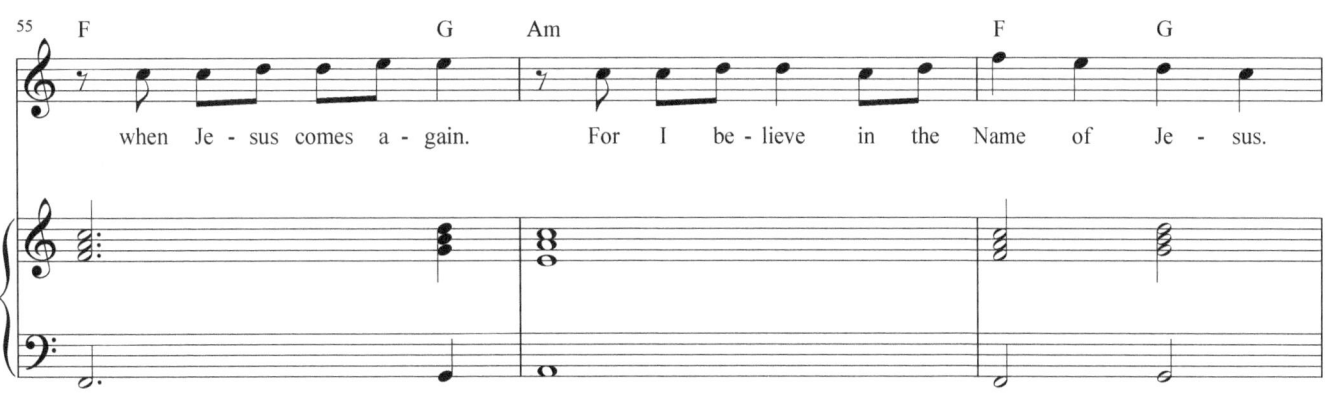

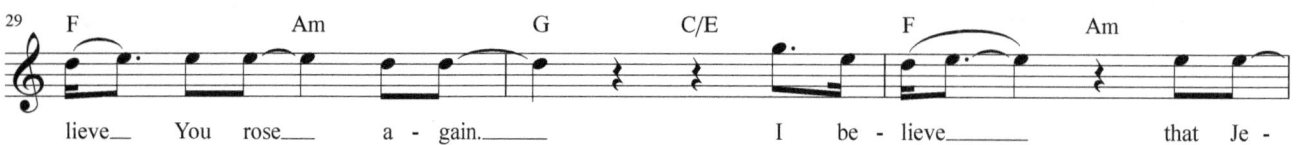
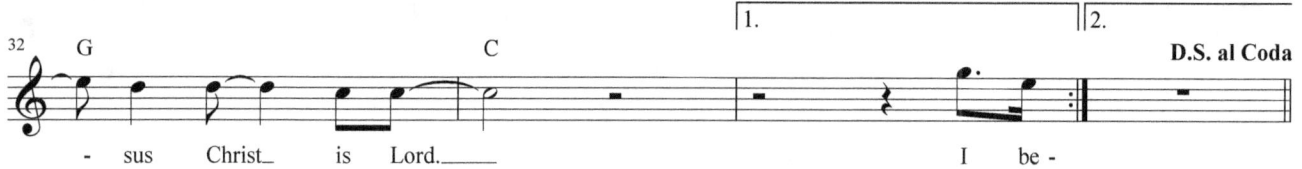

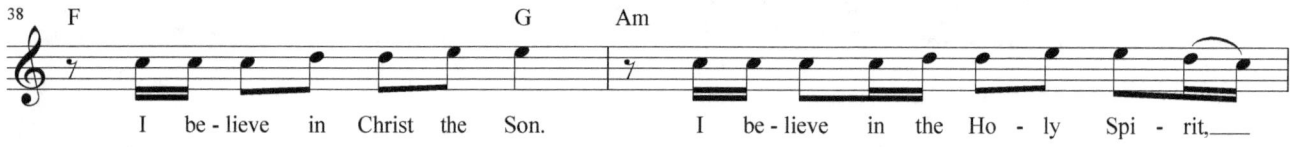
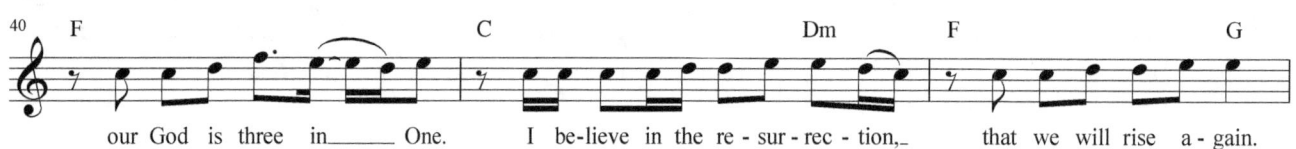
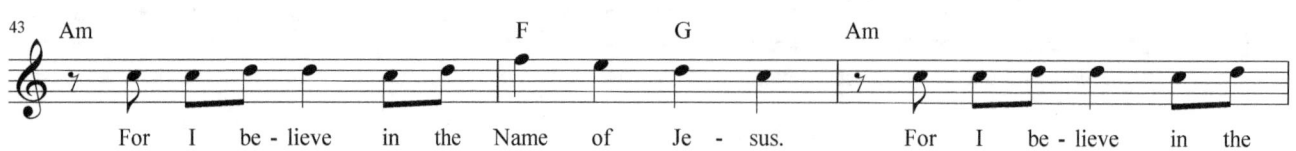

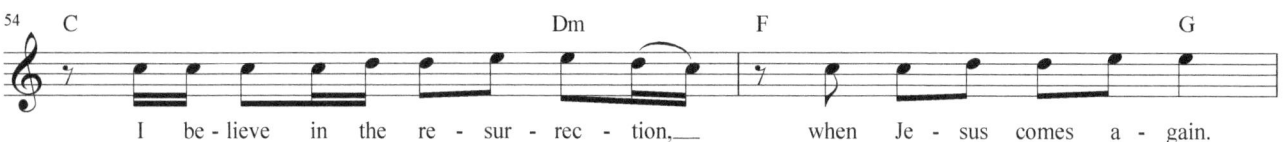
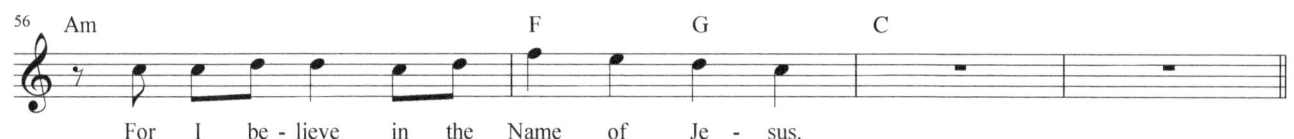

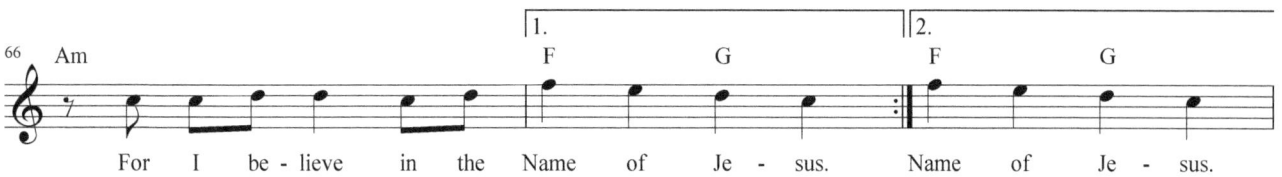
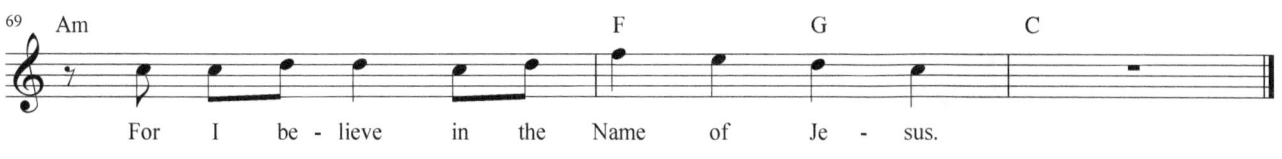

THIS I BELIEVE
(THE CREED)

**Words and Music by
Matt Crocker & Ben Fielding**

VERSE 1:
**Our Father everlasting
The all creating One
God Almighty**

**Through Your Holy Spirit
Conceiving Christ the Son
Jesus our Saviour**

VERSE 2:
**Our Judge and our Defender
Suffered and crucified
Forgiveness is in You**

**Descended into darkness
You rose in glorious life
Forever seated high**

© 2014 Hillsong Music Publishing (APRA).
Used by permission.
Tel: +61 2 8853 5300
Email: publishing@hillsong.com
CCLI Song No. 7018338

CHORUS:
I believe in God our Father
I believe in Christ the Son
I believe in the Holy Spirit
Our God is three in One
I believe in the resurrection
That we will rise again
For I believe
In the Name of Jesus

BRIDGE:
I believe in You
I believe You rose again
I believe that Jesus Christ is Lord

CHORUS 2:
I believe in life eternal
I believe in the virgin birth
I believe in the saints' communion
And in Your holy Church
I believe in the resurrection
When Jesus comes again
For I believe in the Name of Jesus

HEAVEN AND EARTH

Words and Music by
BEN FIELDING & SAM KNOCK

Love that was fore-told___ when the pro-phets___ spoke___
Now He comes with___ hope in sal-va-tion's___ robe___
___ of One to___ come.___
___ to lead us___ home.___

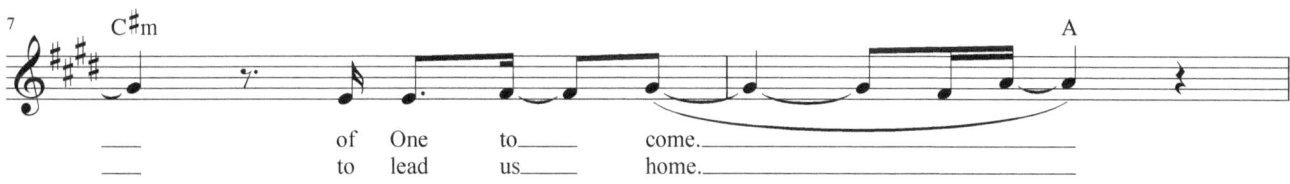

Heav-en came for___ us,___ re-con-cil-ing___ hearts___
Heal-ing in His___ wings,___ free-dom in His___ scars,

___ to You our___ God.___ }
___ His king-dom___ come.___ } Heav-en and earth___

© 2014 Hillsong Music Publishing (APRA).
All rights reserved. International copyright secured. Used by permission.
Tel: +61 2 8853 5300 Email: publishing@hillsong.com CCLI Song No. 7019977

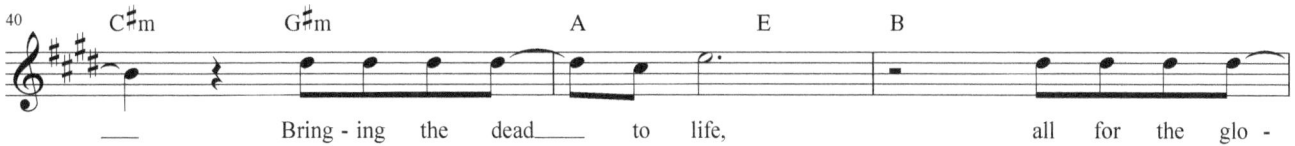
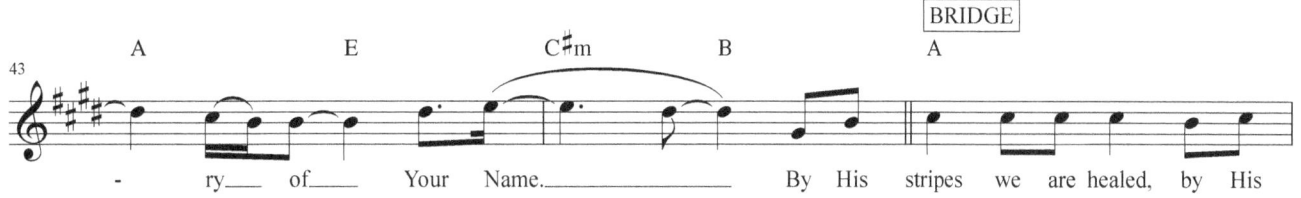

HEAVEN AND EARTH

**Words and Music by
Ben Fielding & Sam Knock**

VERSE 1:
Love that was foretold
When the prophets spoke
Of One to come

Heaven came for us
Reconciling hearts
To You our God

CHORUS:
Heaven and earth collide
The Saviour for everyone has come
Bringing the dead to life
All for the glory of Your Name

© 2014 Hillsong Music Publishing (APRA).
All rights reserved. International copyright secured.
Used by permission.
Tel: +61 2 8853 5300
Email: publishing@hillsong.com
CCLI Song No. 7019977

VERSE 2:
Now He comes with hope
In salvation's robe
To lead us home

Healing in His wings
Freedom in His scars
His kingdom come

BRIDGE:
By His stripes we are healed
By His death we can live
In Jesus' Name
In Jesus' Name
All oppression will cease
Every captive released
In Jesus' Name
In Jesus' Name

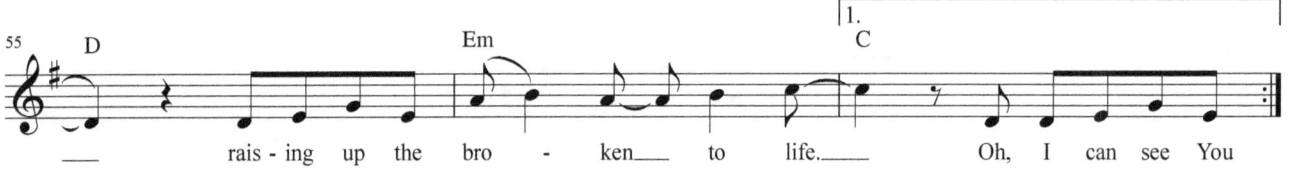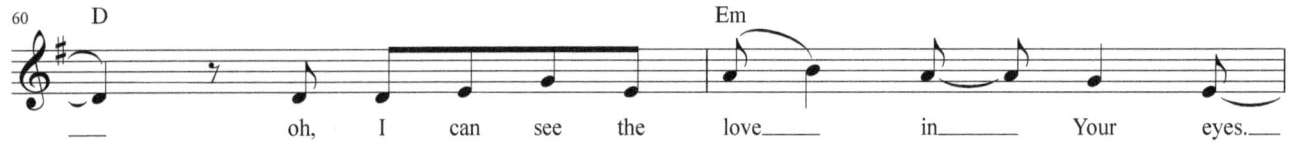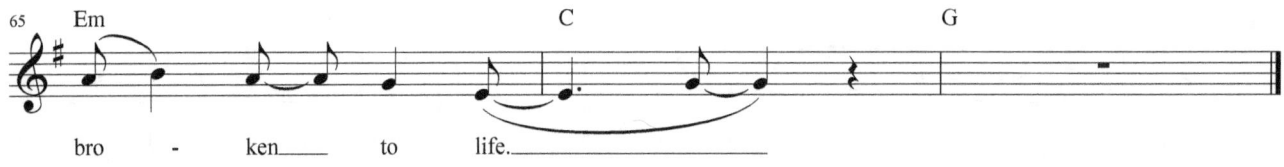

BROKEN VESSELS
(AMAZING GRACE)

**Words and Music by
Joel Houston & Jonas Myrin**

VERSE 1:
All these pieces
Broken and scattered
In mercy gathered
Mended and whole
Empty handed
But not forsaken
I've been set free
I've been set free

PRE-CHORUS:
Amazing grace
How sweet the sound
That saved a wretch like me
I once was lost
But now I am found
Was blind but now I see

© 2014 Hillsong Music Publishing (APRA).
All rights reserved. International copyright secured.
Used by permission.
Tel: +61 2 8853 5300
Email: publishing@hillsong.com
CCLI Song No. 7019974

CHORUS:
Oh I can see You now
Oh I can see the love in Your eyes
Laying Yourself down
Raising up the broken to life

VERSE 2:
You take our failure
You take our weakness
You set Your treasure
In jars of clay
So take this heart Lord
I'll be Your vessel
The world to see Your life in me

NO OTHER NAME

**Words and Music by
JOEL HOUSTON & JONAS MYRIN**

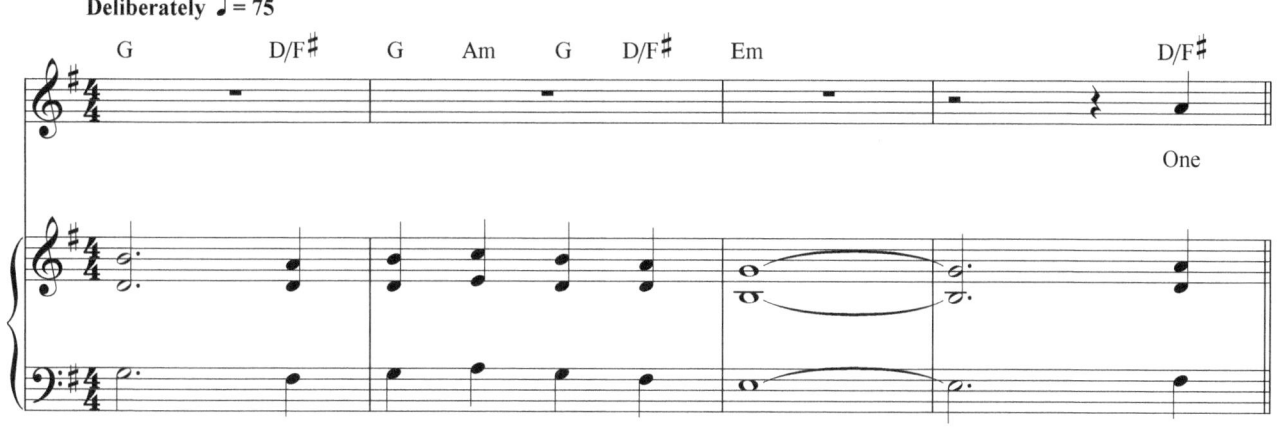

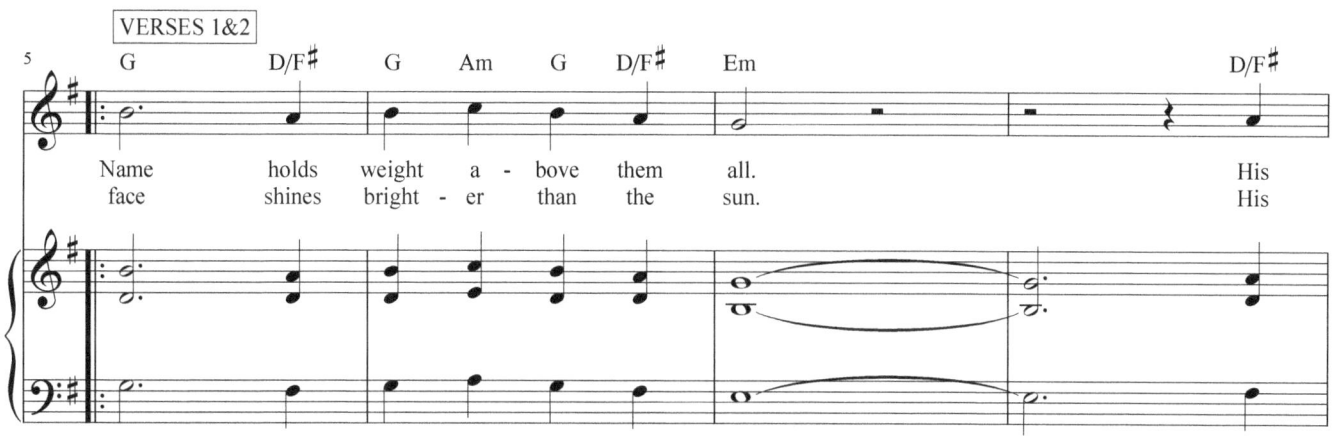

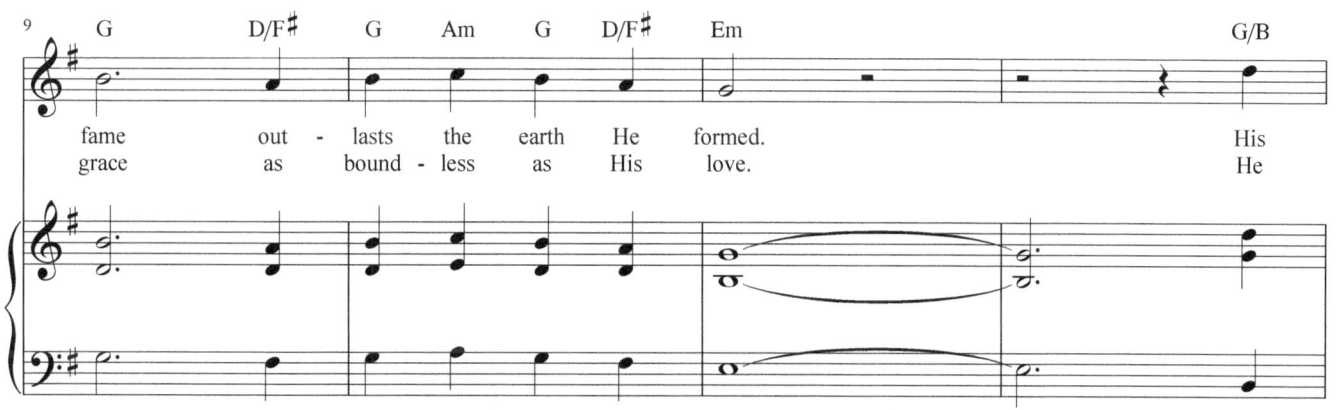

© 2014 Hillsong Music Publishing (APRA).
All rights reserved. International copyright secured. Used by permission.
Tel: +61 2 8853 5300 Email: publishing@hillsong.com CCLI Song No. 7019979

NO OTHER NAME

**Words and Music by
Joel Houston & Jonas Myrin**

VERSE 1:
**One Name
Holds weight above them all
His fame
Outlasts the earth He formed
His praise
Resounds beyond the stars
And echoes in our hearts
The greatest One of all**

VERSE 2:
**His face
Shines brighter than the sun
His grace
As boundless as His love
He reigns
With healing in His wings
The King above all kings
The greatest One of all**

© 2014 Hillsong Music Publishing (APRA).
All rights reserved. International copyright secured.
Used by permission.
Tel: +61 2 8853 5300
Email: publishing@hillsong.com
CCLI Song No. 7019979

CHORUS:
Lift up our eyes see the King has come
Light of the world
Reaching out for us
There is no other Name
There is no other Name
Jesus Christ our God

Seated on high the undefeated One
Mountains bow down as we lift Him up
There is no other Name
There is no other Name
Jesus Christ our God

VERSE 3:
Find hope
When all the world seems lost
Behold
The triumph of the cross
His power has trampled death and grave
Our life found in His Name
The greatest Name of all

BRIDGE:
**The earth will shake
And tremble before Him
Chains will break
As heaven and earth sing
Holy is the Name
Holy is the Name of Jesus Jesus Jesus**

© 2014 Hillsong Music Publishing (APRA).
All rights reserved. International copyright secured.
Used by permission.
Tel: +61 2 8853 5300
Email: publishing@hillsong.com
CCLI Song No. 7019979

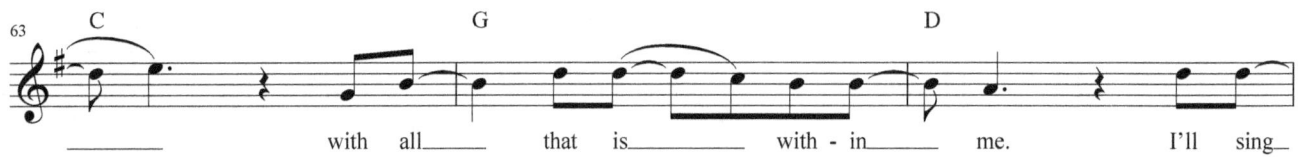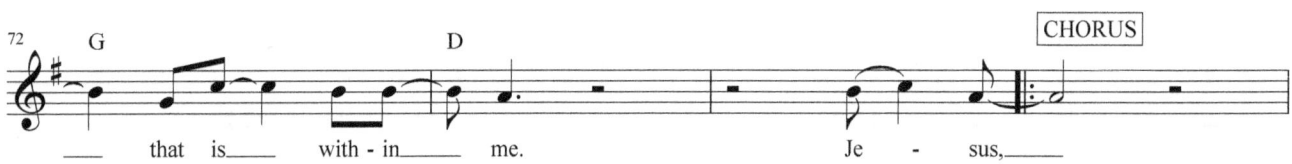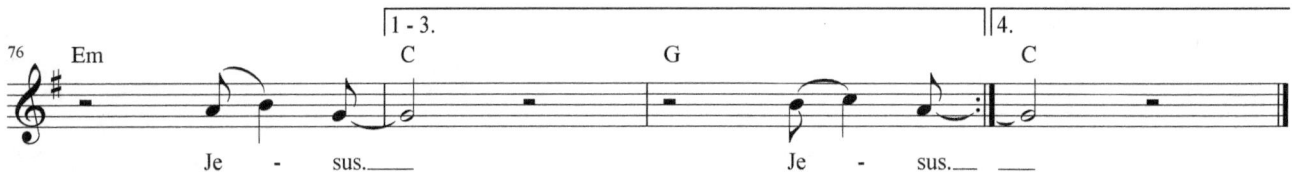

DEPTHS

**Words and Music by
Brooke Ligertwood & Marty Sampson**

VERSE 1:
**In Your presence I quiet my soul
And I hear Your voice
In my spirit I hear the sound
Of salvation's song**

PRE-CHORUS:
**Jesus
Jesus**

Verse 2:
**I will wait in Your word oh Lord
There Your Spirit speaks
Bringing life to the weary soul
To the depths of me**

© 2014 Hillsong Music Publishing (APRA).
All rights reserved. International copyright secured.
Used by permission.
Tel: +61 2 8853 5300
Email: publishing@hillsong.com
CCLI Song No. 7019976

BRIDGE:
I love You with all my heart
I love You with all my soul Lord
I love You with all my strength
With all that is within me

I'll sing 'cause You saved my soul I'll sing of Your love forever
I'll worship with all my heart With all that is within me

CALVARY

(Inspired by "Calvary Covers It All" – by Mrs. Walter G. Taylor)

Words and Music by
REUBEN MORGAN & JONAS MYRIN

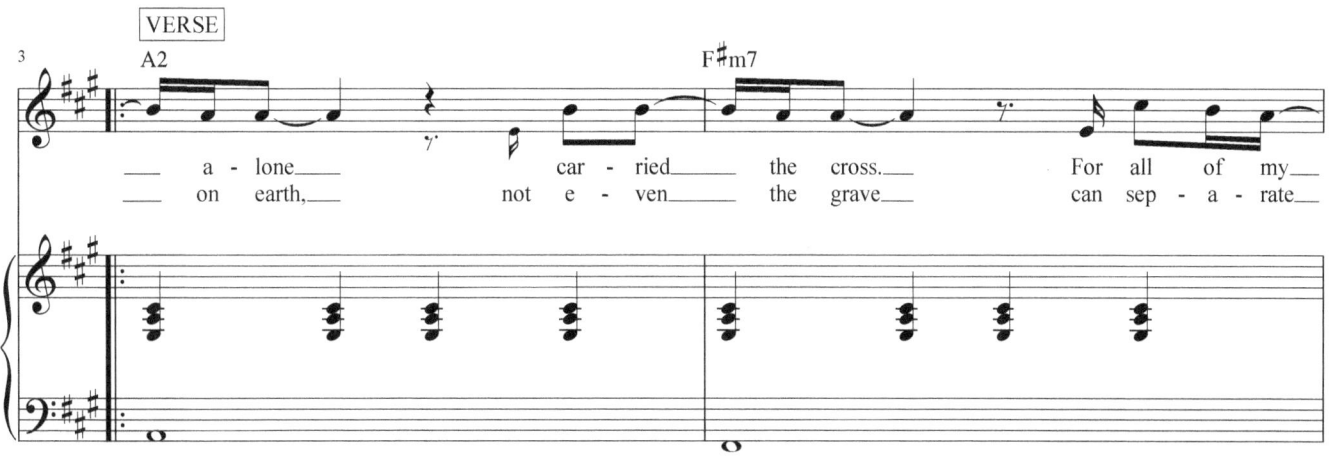

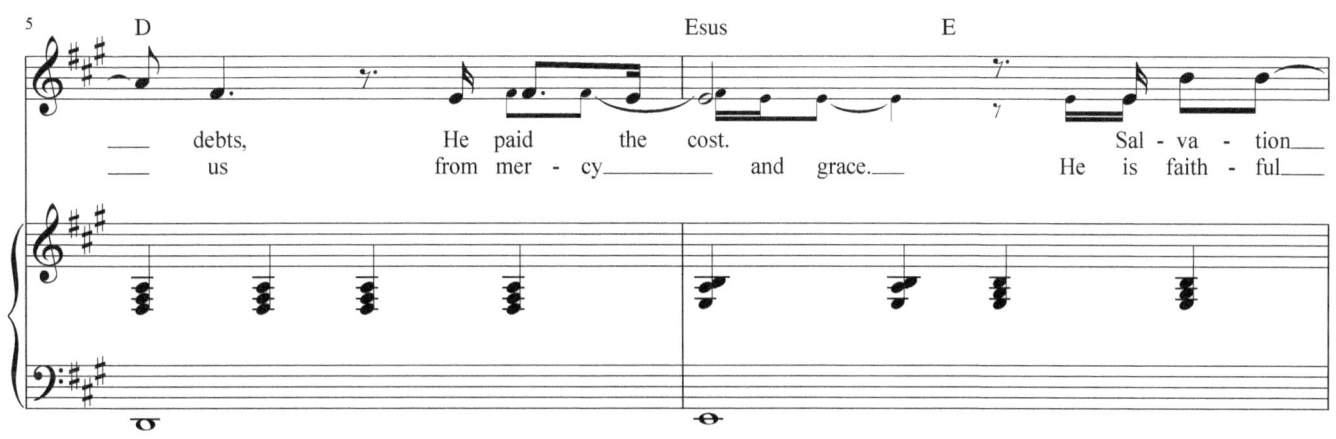

© 2014 Hillsong Music Publishing (admin in USA and Canada by Capitol Music Group, Word Music, LLC (a div. of Word Music Group, Inc.)
All rights reserved. International copyright secured. Used by permission.
Tel: +61 2 8853 5300 Email: publishing@hillsong.com CCLI Song No. 7018337

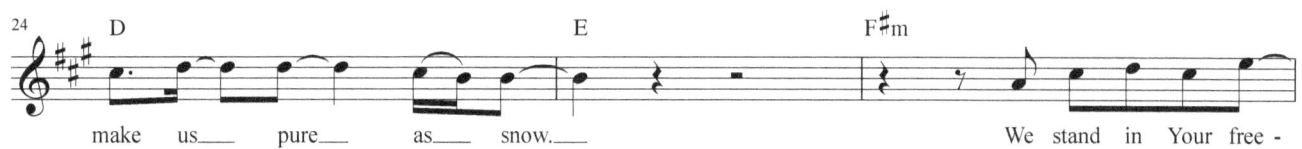
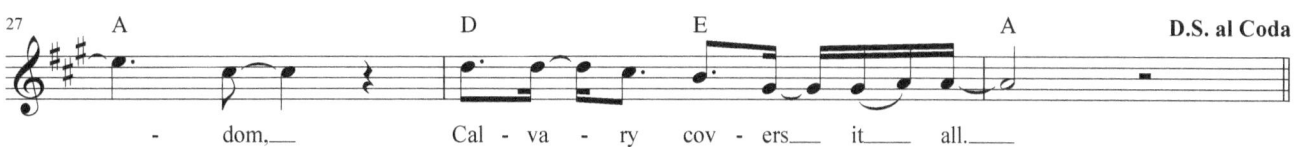
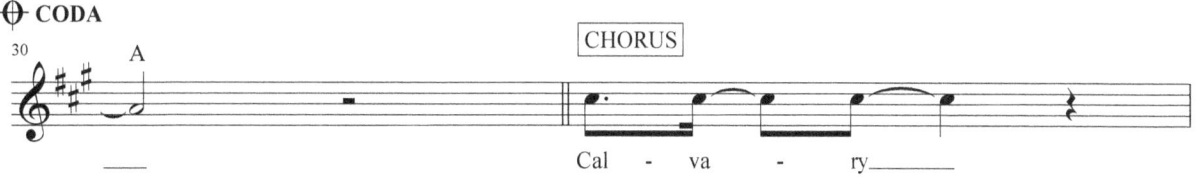

CALVARY

**Words and Music by
Reuben Morgan & Jonas Myrin**

VERSE 1:
**The Saviour alone
Carried the cross
For all of my debts
He paid the cost
Salvation complete
Forever I'm free
Calvary covers it all**

CHORUS:
**Calvary covers it all
My sin and shame
Don't count anymore
All praise to the One
Who has ransomed my soul
Calvary covers it all**

Inspired by "Calvary Covers It All" – by Mrs. Walter G. Taylor

© 2014 Hillsong Music Publishing (APRA).
All rights reserved. International copyright secured.
Used by permission.
Tel: +61 2 8853 5300
Email: publishing@hillsong.com
CCLI Song No. 7018337

VERSE 2:
**No power on earth
Not even the grave
Can separate us
From mercy and grace
He is faithful to save
Oh His blood never fails
Calvary covers it all**

BRIDGE:
**No one but Jesus
Can make us pure as snow
We stand in Your freedom
Calvary covers it all**

THANK YOU JESUS

Words and Music by
MATT CROCKER & HANNAH HOBBS

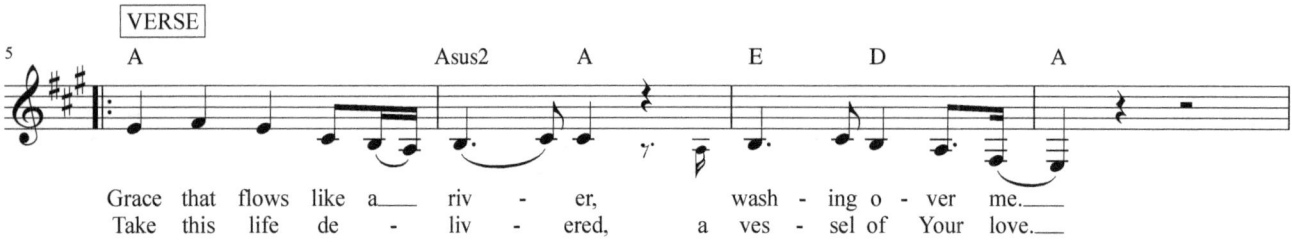

Grace that flows like a river, washing over me.
Take this life delivered, a vessel of Your love.

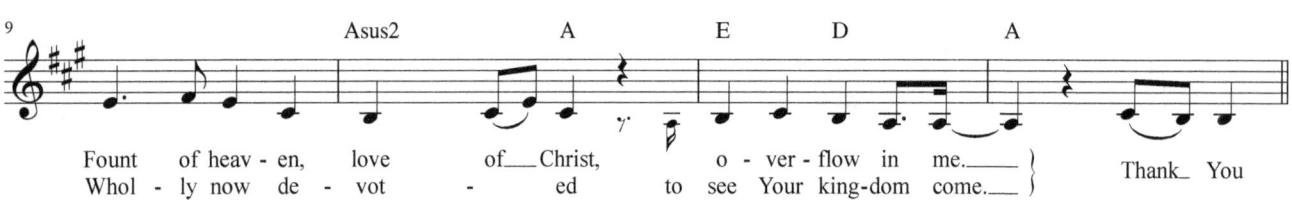

Fount of heaven, love of Christ, overflow in me. ⎱ Thank You
Wholly now devoted to see Your kingdom come. ⎰

CHORUS

Jesus, You set me free. Christ my

Saviour, You rescued me.

Thank You Jesus, You set me free.

© 2013 Hillsong Music Publishing (APRA).
All rights reserved. International copyright secured. Used by permission.
Tel: +61 2 8853 5300 Email: publishing@hillsong.com CCLI Song No. 7004672

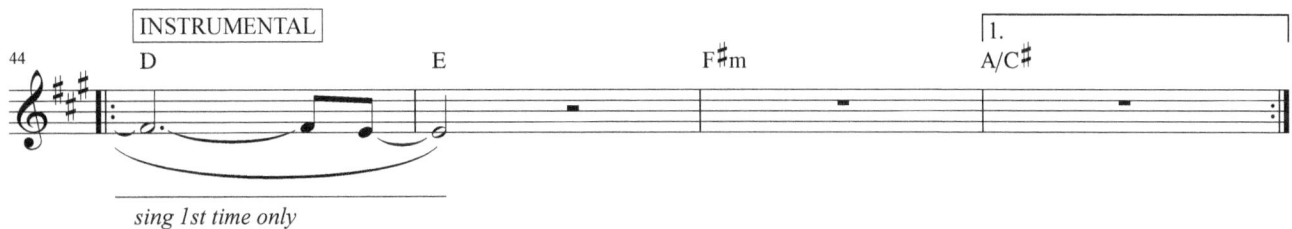

sing 1st time only

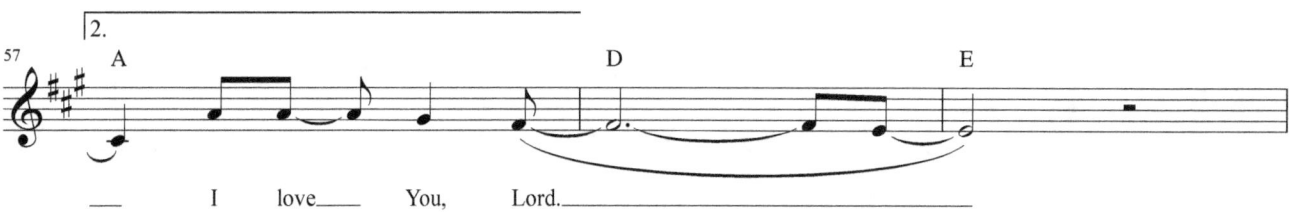

THANK YOU JESUS

**Words and Music by
Matt Crocker & Hannah Hobbs**

VERSE 1:
**Grace that flows like a river
Washing over me
Fount of heaven
Love of Christ
Overflow in me**

CHORUS:
**Thank You Jesus
You set me free
Christ my Saviour
You rescued me**

VERSE 2:
**Take this life delivered
A vessel of Your love
Wholly now devoted
To see Your kingdom come**

© 2013 Hillsong Music Publishing (APRA).
All rights reserved. International copyright secured.
Used by permission.
Tel: +61 2 8853 5300
Email: publishing@hillsong.com
CCLI Song No. 7004672

TAG:
**You've given me life
You've opened my eyes
I love You Lord
I love You Lord**

**You've entered my heart
You've set me apart
I love You Lord
I love You Lord**

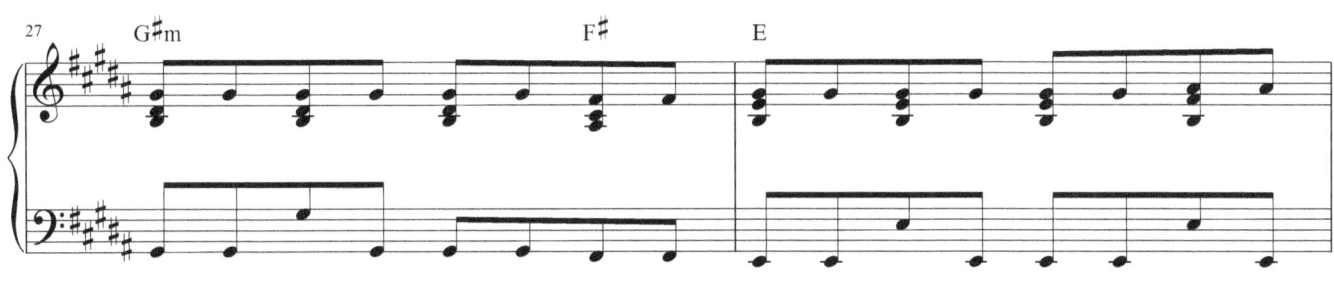

The heav - ens have been

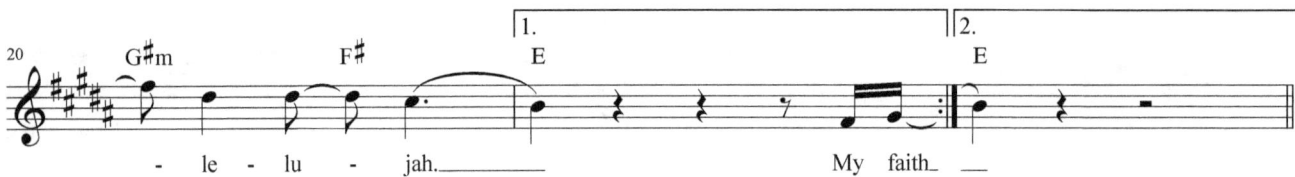

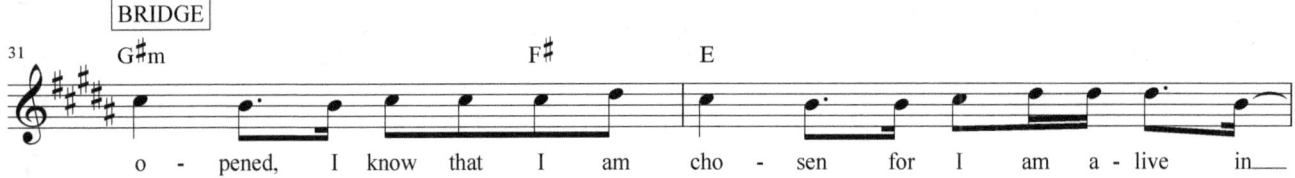
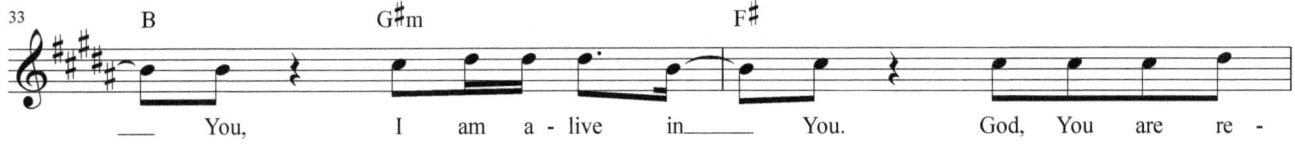

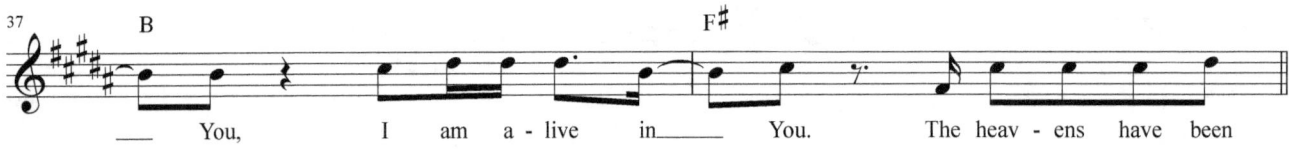

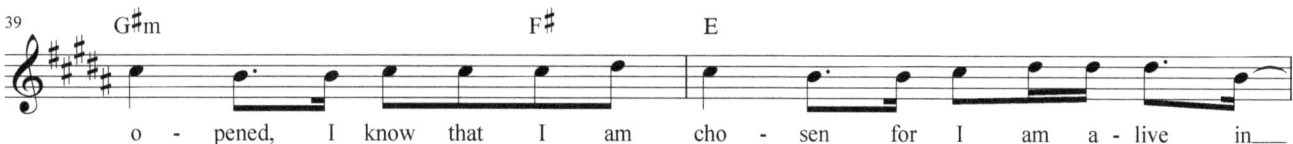

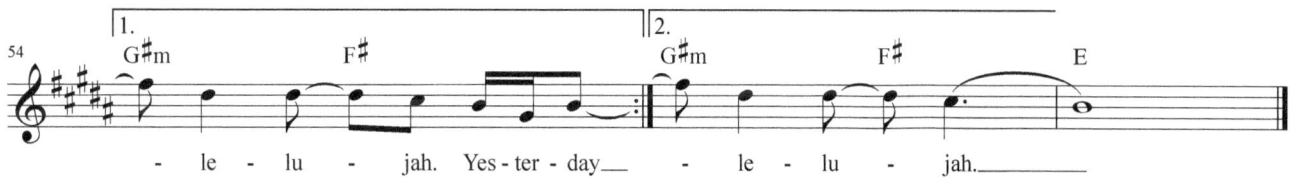

ALL THINGS NEW

**Words and Music by
Ben Fielding & Dean Ussher**

VERSE 1:
Your love's making all things new You're working in all for good
For the things of this world
There is hope renewed
In the life that is found in You

VERSE 2:
My faith is in things unseen
Bringing life where it has not been
Speaking things that are not
As if they were
I am alive in You

© 2013 Hillsong Music Publishing (APRA).
All rights reserved. International copyright secured.
Used by permission.
Tel: +61 2 8853 5300
Email: publishing@hillsong.com
CCLI Song No. 7019975

CHORUS:
**You make all things new
You make all things new
Yesterday and forever
Your love never changing This hope never fading Hallelujah**

BRIDGE:
**The heavens have been opened I know that I am chosen
I am alive in You
I am alive in You**

**God You are restoring All things for Your glory I am alive in You
I am alive in You**

MY STORY

Words and Music by
REUBEN MORGAN & JARRAD ROGERS

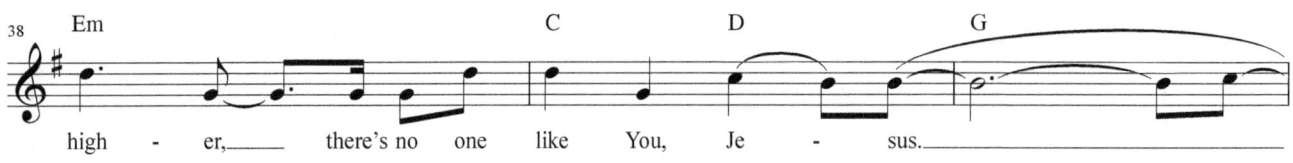
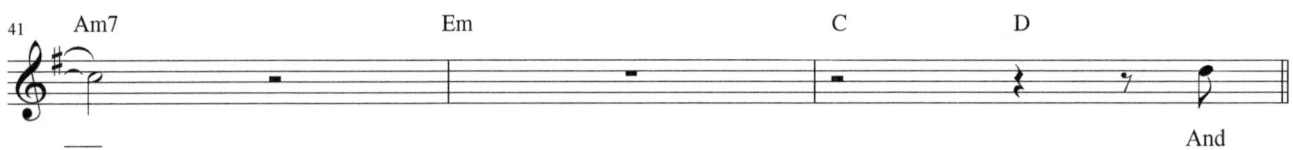

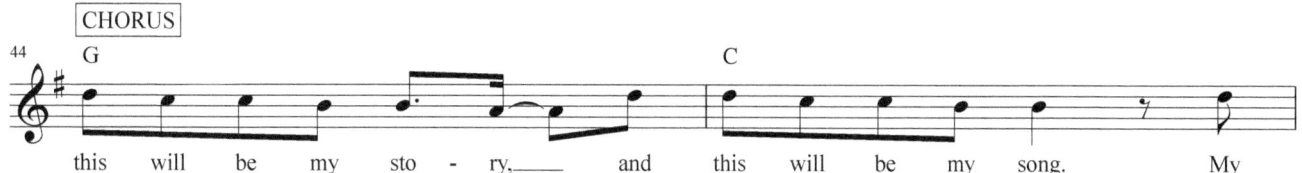

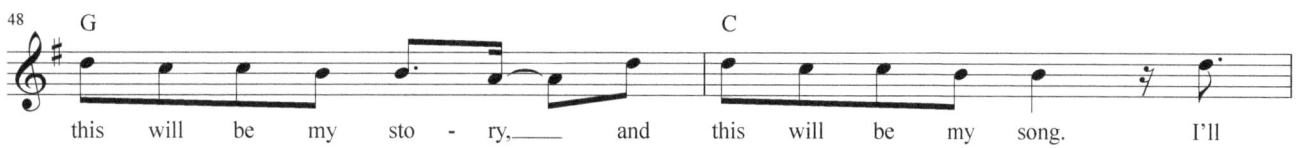

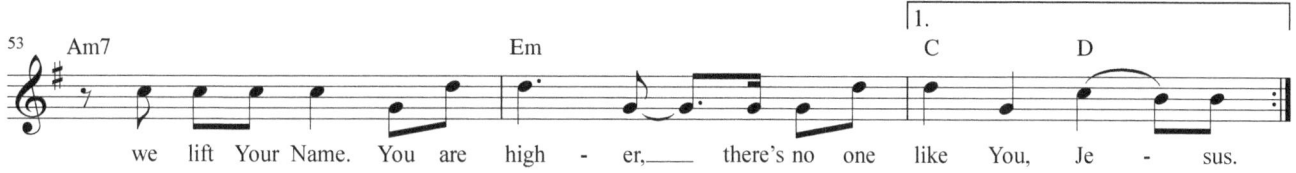

MY STORY

**Words and Music by
Reuben Morgan & Jarrad Rogers**

VERSE 1:
God will always be my strength
Nothing less than Christ my Saviour
God will always be my hope
Nothing more than Christ alone

CHORUS:
And this will be my story
And this will be my song
My chains are broken
I am free
And this will be my story
And this will be my song
I'll praise You my Saviour
Jesus

© 2014 Hillsong Music Publishing (APRA) & Imagem
Music Publishing UK
All rights reserved. International copyright secured.
Used by permission.
Tel: +61 2 8853 5300
Email: publishing@hillsong.com
CCLI Song No. 7019978

VERSE 2:
Take my life but give me Jesus
To know You God is why I live
Take the world but give me Jesus
For all my days
I'll follow You

BRIDGE:
We lift Your Name up
We lift Your Name
You are higher
There's no one like You
Jesus

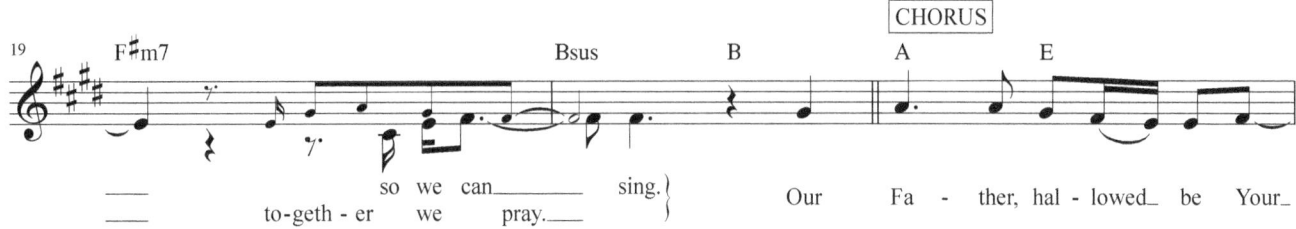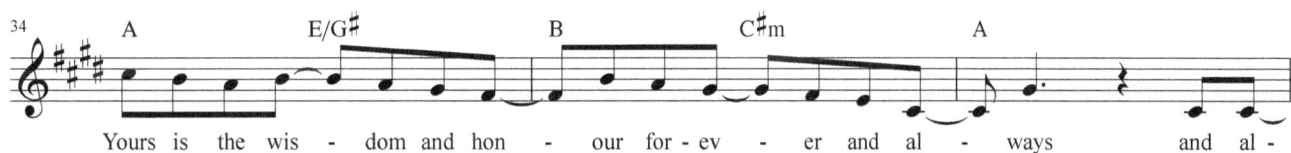

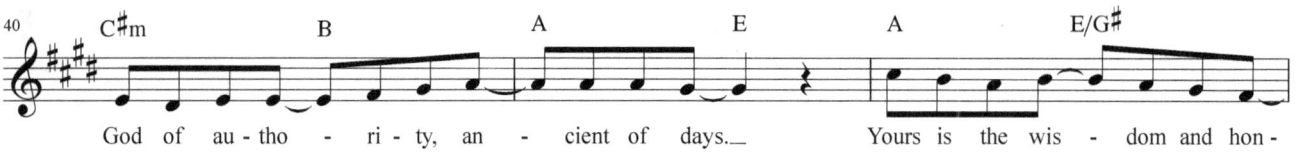

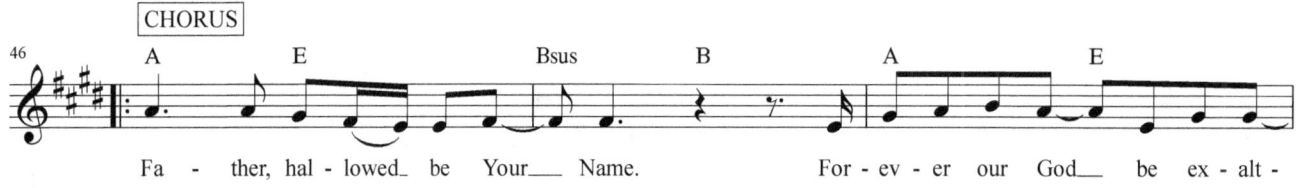

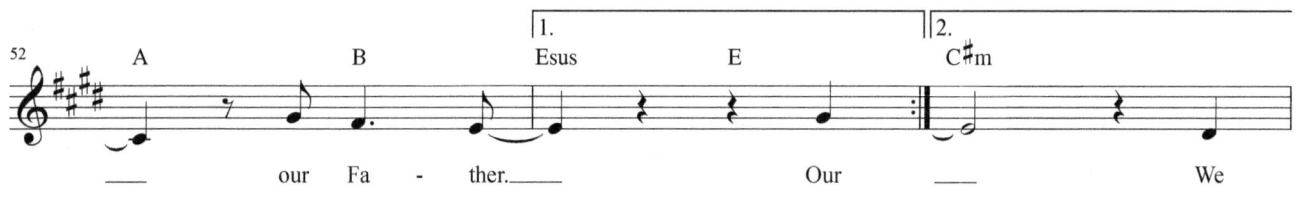

OUR FATHER

Words and Music by Brooke Ligertwood,
Scott Ligertwood & Jonas Myrin

VERSE 1:
The words of Christ
Passed down through generations
The Son of God teaching us to pray
Echoed words
Father have Your will Your way in me
Completely

VERSE 2:
We wholly trust
You're faithful in provision
Amazing grace mercy for our sins
May we forgive
The way that You've forgiven us oh Lord
So we can sing

© 2014 Hillsong Music Publishing (APRA).
All rights reserved. International copyright secured.
Used by permission.
Tel: +61 2 8853 5300
Email: publishing@hillsong.com
CCLI Song No. 7019980

CHORUS:
Our Father
Hallowed be Your Name
Forever our God be exalted
Your kingdom come and in us
Let Your will be done
Our Father

VERSE 3:
Lead us from the valley of temptation
Deliver us from the evil one
Lord You reign and here we stand Victorious in Your Name
Together we pray

BRIDGE:
Yours is the kingdom and power and glory
God of authority ancient of days
Yours is the wisdom and honour
Forever and always
We pray

MOUNTAIN

Words and Music by
MATT CROCKER & JOEL HOUSTON

Building, with momentum ♩ = 79

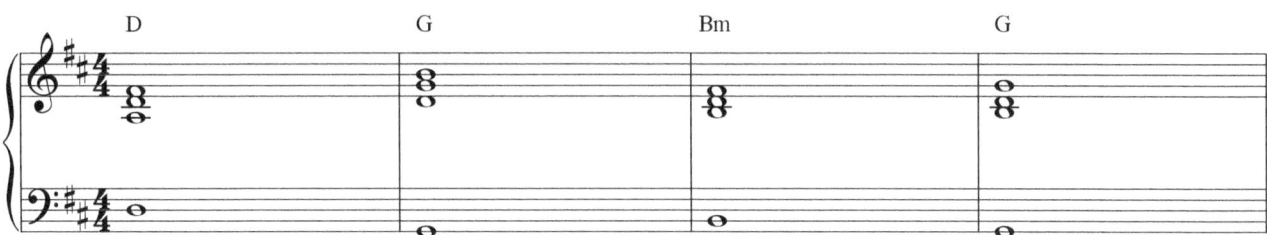

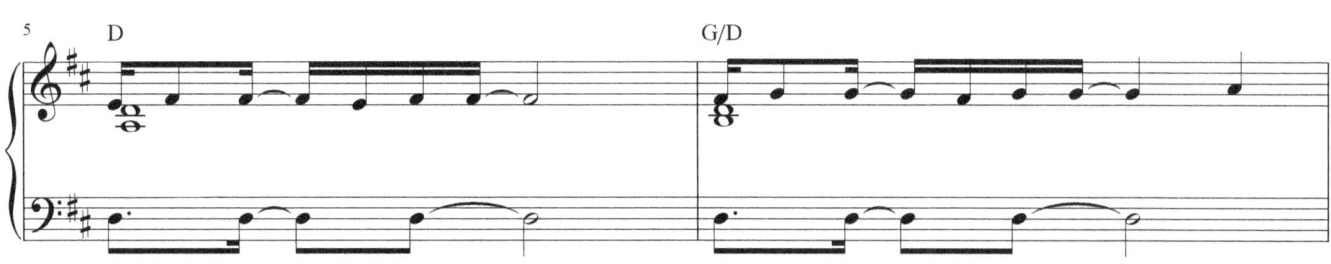

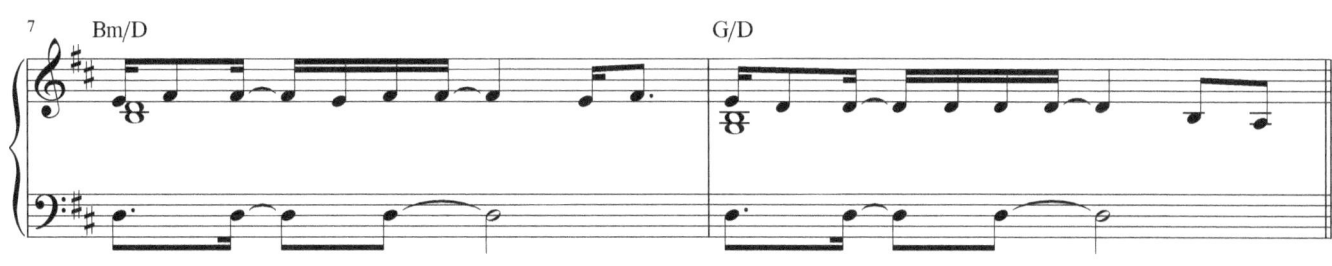

VERSE

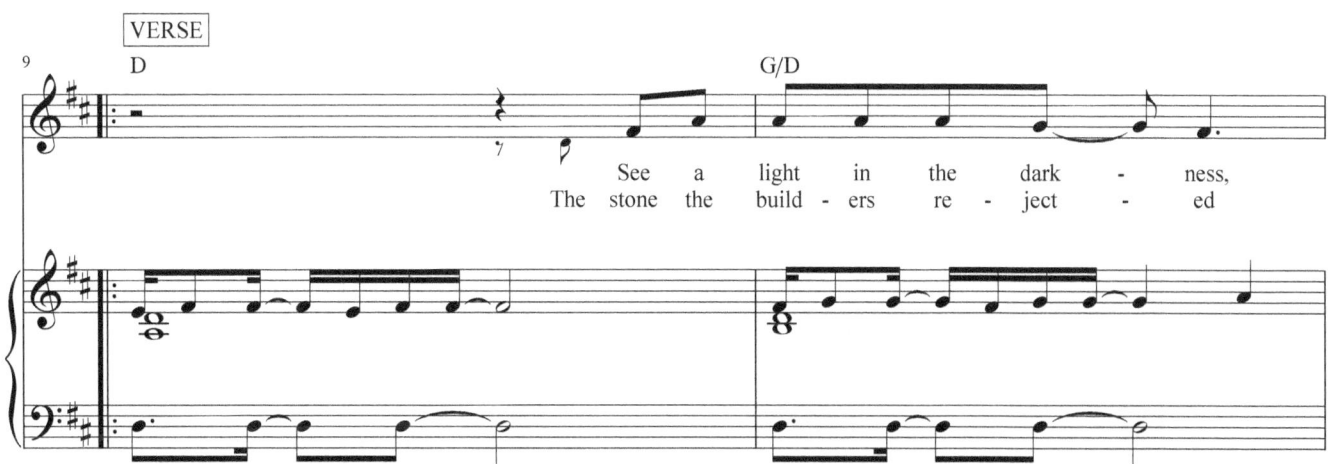

See a light in the darkness,
The stone the build-ers re-ject-ed

© 2012 Hillsong Music Publishing (APRA).
All rights reserved. International copyright secured. Used by permission.
Tel: +61 2 8853 5300 Email: publishing@hillsong.com CCLI Song No. 6428853

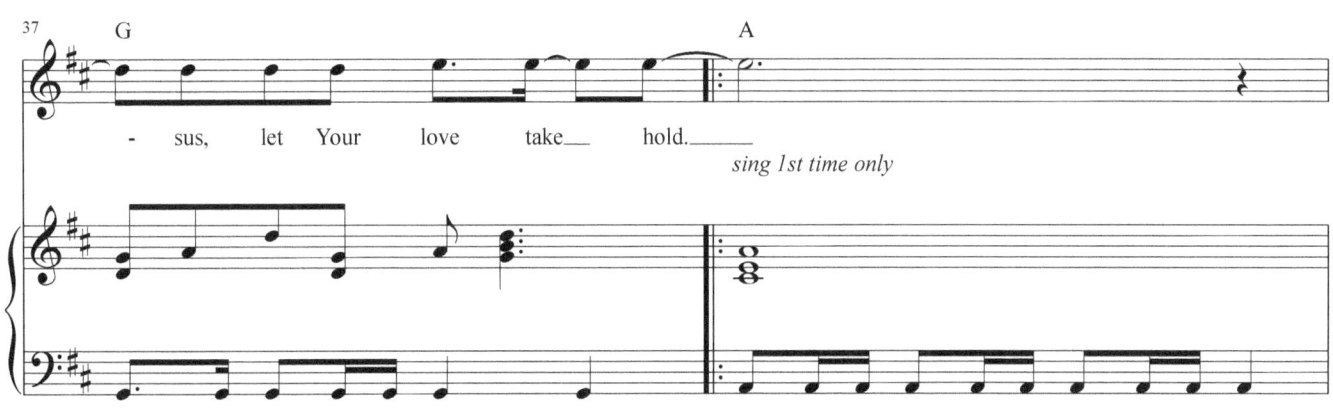

MOUNTAIN

Words and Music by
MATT CROCKER & JOEL HOUSTON

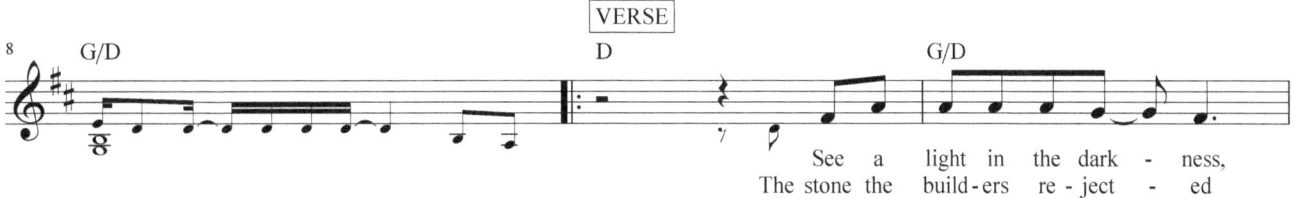
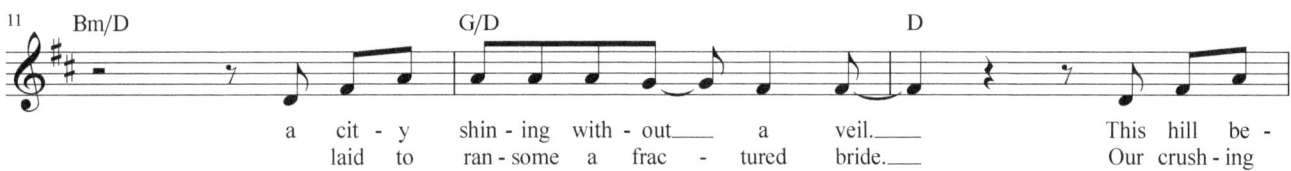
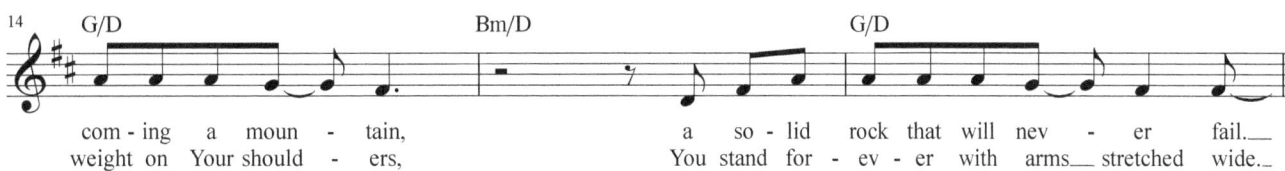
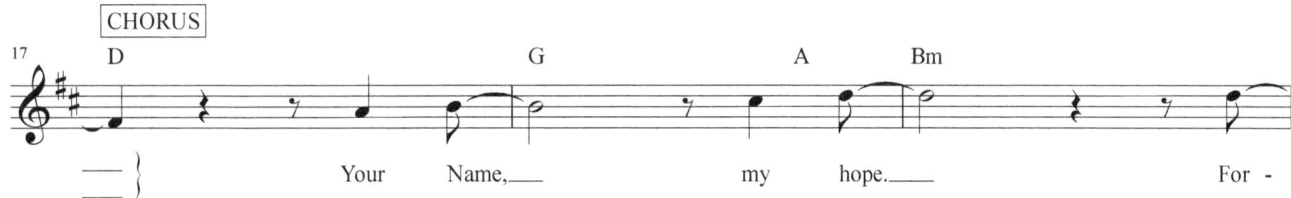

© 2012 Hillsong Music Publishing (APRA).
All rights reserved. International copyright secured. Used by permission.
Tel: +61 2 8853 5300 Email: publishing@hillsong.com CCLI Song No. 6428853

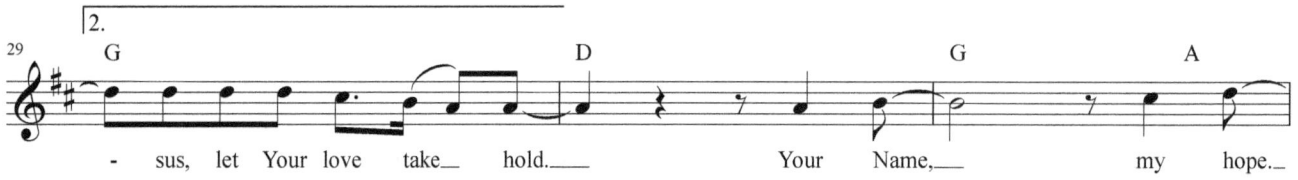

sing 1st time only

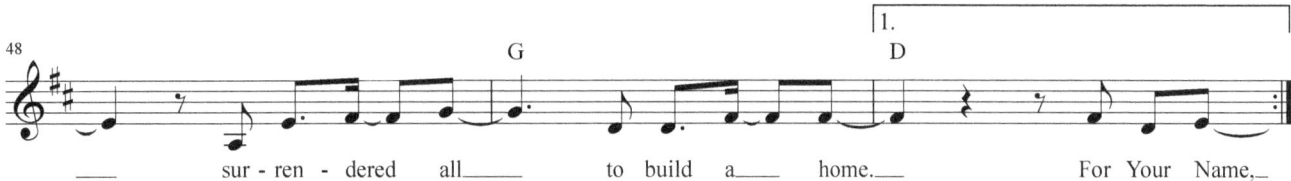

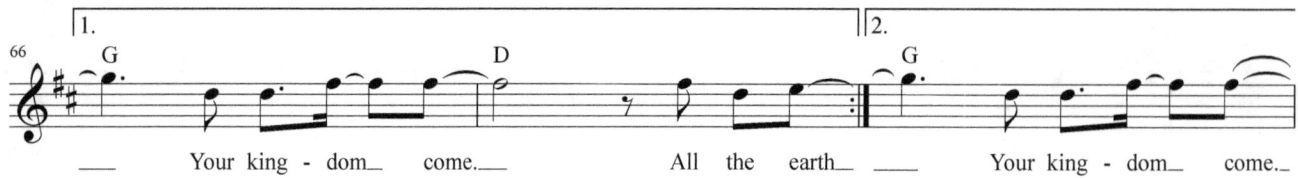

MOUNTAIN

**Words and Music by
Matt Crocker & Joel Houston**

VERSE 1:
See a light in the darkness
A city shining without a veil
This hill becoming a mountain
A solid rock that will never fail

CHORUS:
Your Name my hope
Fortress in the raging storm
My heart is Your home
Jesus let Your love take hold

VERSE 2:
The Stone the builders rejected
Laid to ransom a fractured bride
Our crushing weight on Your shoulders
You stand forever with arms stretched wide

© 2012 Hillsong Music Publishing (APRA).
All rights reserved. International copyright secured.
Used by permission.
Tel: +61 2 8853 5300
Email: publishing@hillsong.com
CCLI Song No. 6428853

BRIDGE 1:
For Your Name
Heart and soul
My life is Yours a living stone
For Your glory
Heart and soul
Surrendered all to build a home

BRIDGE 2:
Your Name my sure foundation
The Hope of glory for one and all
Your love endures forever
A holy mountain that will not fall

BRIDGE 3:
All the earth welcome home
In every heart Your will be done
All creation welcome home
This hope is ours
Your kingdom come

BRIDGE 4:
We cry holy holy holy
We cry holy is Your Name